Y0-CUX-410

Chichester Remembered
A Pictorial Past

©Kenneth Green 1989

All rights reserved. No part of this book may be reproduced or transmitted in any form or by any means, electronic or mechanical, including photocopying, recording or any information storage and retrieval system without permission in writing from the publishers excepting brief passages used in review.

This first edition published in 1989 by
ENSIGN Publications
2 Redcar Street
Southampton SO1 5LL

ISBN 185455 013 6

British Library Cataloguing in Publication Data
Green, Kenneth, 1932 –
Chichester: a pictorial past.
1. West Sussex, history
I. Title
942.2'62

Designed by Mark Eslick
Edited by David Graves
Typeset by Alphaset

Chichester Remembered
A Pictorial Past

Kenneth Green

Ensign
PUBLICATIONS

INTRODUCTION

Although Chichester is a historic City it does not have a very significant place in history. An adequate history book of the country could be written without one mention of Chichester. It is, I believe, precisely this lack of past prominence that makes Chichester important to historians. The City has no doubt been affected by all of the events of the past and yet it has not contributed an event which has proved significant in altering the course of history itself. By studying its history we can therefore get a picture of the lives of ordinary men and women, I feel it is essential that we try to set down all we can of how it was in our time, that which represents the remembered past of Chichester.

When researching the past, especially in a City as ancient as Chichester, it is easy to overlook the happenings of recent times. The reception given to my first book, 'Chichester Past and Present', made it clear that there is great interest in life as it was in the City in the not so distant past.

Whereas in the earlier book the aim was to compare past street scenes with those of today, I have this time used a compendium approach with photographs and reminiscences of what was a very closely knit community. I have gathered material and received help from many people and a wide variety of sources, I am glad that many share my enthusiasm for recording a Chichester that so many remember with such affection.

Alterations to the City have taken place, often without them being especially noticed at the time, it is often not until one is reminded, by looking at photographs or listening to some of the older residents, that one appreciates the extent of the changes. I have concentrated on those areas where change is most apparent, such as shops, pubs, churches, etc. Also included are many photographs that show events and grand occasions from the City's past.

Among the more noticeable transformations in street scenes of any town, over a period of years, are the changes that take place in the ownership of the shops and in the types of business carried on in them. I think it appropriate that there are many pictures in this collection that emphasise this aspect of change.

In Chichester many old established family firms, some that were founded in Victorian times, have gone, the shops that have replaced them do not always have the same durability, some have disappeared within months of their opening, building societies and estate agencies seem to have taken over many of the premises. Notwithstanding these changes shopping in the City still has something to offer that modern towns seem to lack.

The shopkeepers in the past were often respected characters in a City, one only has to look through a list of former Mayors of Chichester to see the part they played in civic affairs. A seat on the City Corporation was a position of local importance, the Corporation was responsible for the administration of many public facilities including the Market, the Cemetery and the Fire Brigade as well as the upkeep of the roads, street lighting, council housing, drains and the Sewage Works. They also supplied gas, water and electricity to the City.

The Corporation was made up from eighteen councillors, six elected from each of the three City wards, and six aldermen, chosen by the councillors usually, but not necessarily, from among their number. Councillors held office for three years before coming up for re-election and the aldermen six. The Mayor held office for one year at a time being elected by the full Corporation.

Most of the aldermen also served the community as J.P.s on the local Bench and many of their names were to be found on the governing boards of schools, hospitals, and other official bodies.

By and large it was only the businessmen and the well-to-do that could afford either the time or the expense of taking part in civic affairs, but this should not diminish the credit due them for their, mostly unrewarded, efforts.

The City of Chichester in the years before the last war had changed little since the turn of the Century, the pace of life was much slower, those that can remember the scenes shown in this book have had to appreciate two very different periods of history. We should be thankful that there were photographers, both amateur and professional, whose foresight in recording everyday scenes and occurrences has given us this revealing glimpse of the recent past.

As with the earlier volume, the first object is to entertain and secondly to remind us all of how fortunate we are to live in a place of such character and beauty. I hope it will also show how important it is that we monitor all proposals for change carefully, to make sure that the best features of the City are preserved for future generations.

CONTENTS

Introduction	Page 4
1	Shops and Shopkeepers	6
2	Charlie Howard. Sportsman, Butcher	20
3	Electric Cinemas	22
4	Advertisements	25
5	Street Scenes	27
6	Garages	33
7	The Italian Ice Cream Man	Page 38
8	A Walk Down East Street	40
9	Last Orders at the Bar	49
10	The City's Lost Churches	54
11	The City Celebrates	59
12	Chichester's Postal Past	70
13	Treasure Trove	74

ACKNOWLEDGEMENTS

To compile a book such as this it is necessary to borrow a great many photographs to glean information and to check facts, this would not be possible without the co-operation and assistance of a great many people.

I would like to acknowledge everyone who has helped me over the past eighteen months, I thank them all. They include Mrs Mary Bunn, Miss Goody Ballard, Mrs Freda Patterson, Mrs Chitty, Leslie Holden, Wally Dew, Martin Guarnaccio, Ann Bone and Rosemary Gilmour of the Chichester Museum, Ian McCrae, Andrew Berriman, Don and Mollie Bowers, Peter and Grace Briant, and the late Bill Walton.

Special thanks also to David Graves of Ensign Publications for technical advice and support.

And of course to Sheila, my wife, for her patience and encouragement.

SHOPS AND SHOPKEEPERS

▲ What better way to start this section than with a photograph of two well respected Chichester concerns that were typical of the small businesses that abounded in the City. Harry Turner was a boot and shoemaker in the days when, for the well to do, it was the recognised practice to have their footwear made to measure. Harry was a keen member of the Priory Park Bowling club and president of the City Club. When he retired his son Colin ran the business which changed hands after his death in 1964. Still trading in the name of its founder it is one of the few shops that has retained its shopfront from the beginning of the Century.

Mr Denyer was also a well known shopkeeper, still remembered by many. Following the custom in haberdashery shops of the time he would greet customers at his doorway and enquire of their needs, he would then summon the assistant who dealt with that particular commodity, many young Chichester ladies had cause to blush at his loud cry of "Forward Miss Jones, with Bloomers!"

▶ In Eastgate Square, on the North side is a new building comprising shops with flats over, the name of the building is 'Sharp Garland House'. In St Pancras Church nearby there are two plaques that commemorate the lives of Sharp Garland and his son Sir Sharp Archibald Garland, both former churchwardens of the parish. Sharp Garland's shop in Eastgate Square was reputed, at the time of its demolition, to have been the oldest grocery shop in the Country. It was founded by John Smith in 1665. After being in the Hardham family for a hundred years it was bought by Sharp Garland in 1860, he died in 1906 having been a J.P., an Alderman and twice Mayor of the City. His son, Sir Sharp Archibald Garland, also held office, he was Mayor from 1911-18 and in 1920 was made a Freeman of Chichester. He lived at No 10, St John's Street, now occupied by Stride and Son, the Estate Agents and auctioneers.

I have spoken to Miss Goody Ballard, Sir Sharp's niece, who still lives in Chichester. She recalls that he was the first person in Chichester to own a car and remembers it as a large, white open vehicle with red leather upholstery, he died in 1937. The Shop closed and was demolished in 1964. The photograph was taken in 1921, the vehicle shown was the first used for rural deliveries.

▶ Bunns were an institution in Chichester. George Bunn came to Chichester in 1920, he had been a horse dealer in Essex before the 1914-18 War and during it served in the Veterinary Corps. Afterwards there was a slump in farming and with the growing popularity of the motor car the trade in horses became virtually non-existent. After looking in vain for suitable premises he set up in business selling fruit and vegetables from a stall in Baffins Lane. In 1925 he was able to move to a nearby shop on the corner of East Street.

The business thrived and expanded into a major wholesaler of fruit and vegetables, they were also the local distributors for Empire bananas which would be delivered from the Southampton docks by rail. The bananas arrived in a green state and were stored in heated cellars below East Street for ripening. Whilst Mr Bunn controlled the wholesale and buying aspect of the business, his eldest son, also named George, looked after the shop, he joined his father in 1928 aged 14.

During the last war George Bunn, Junior, served on the Ministry of Food committee controlling the supply of vegetables to the West Sussex area. The business closed in 1960 when it was decided to concentrate on the family's other enterprise, owning as it did one of the largest Caravan sites in the Country, at Selsey. The East Street premises were let to Wains who continued with a fruiterers shop there for several years before leaving. Since then the shop has been occupied by several enterprises, none of which seem to last long. The freehold of the premises is still in Bunn family ownership. Douglas Bunn, youngest son of the original owner has carried on the family interest in horses when he became an internationally known show jumper representing England on several occasions. Today he is better known as the Master of Hickstead, The All England Showjumping Centre.

7

▼ Also seen in the last photograph was Harry Wilkins' shop, another shopkeeper who had been on the site since the 1920s when he had taken the business over from Mrs Elsie Ballard. On the right of this picture of his Christmas display in 1922 stands Mr Charlie Foster, it is interesting to note how little the shopfront had changed in forty years.

▲ Harris and Hall, also known as the Central Supply Stores, were grocers, their shop was in East Street at the other end from Sharp Garlands who were their great competitors. They had coffee machines that vented the aroma of the roasting beans out into East Street, they also sold their own exclusive brand of Ceylon Tea. Like all grocers of the time they would deliver goods to customers at no extra charge. Former customers have related to me how there were always chairs in the shop so that one could sit whilst assistants made up the order. Sugar was weighed from sacks and tea from foil lined chests, cheese and bacon being cut to order, shopping was a leisurely activity in those days, at least for the customer. The shop was also an off license, deliveries being made the same day by errand boys on bikes, or in the outlying villages by horse drawn vehicle. I think this picture must have been taken, possibly for the agents selling Harris and Hall, on a Sunday morning. Note the policeman on point duty at the Cross, there had been one there for over thirty years, when it was decided to remove him the traffic seemed to flow more quickly and easily.

Different shops evoke different memories, when I see this picture of Byerley's in East Street I remember the war time queues that formed outside to buy fish, one of the few edible commodities not 'on ration'.

The first picture, like that of Wilkins' shown on an earlier page, shows the Christmas display in 1922, the owner, seen in the centre was Mr T. Kimbell. As with Wilkins, we see a 1960 picture of the business just before it closed in East Street, it was transferred to South Street, it is still there now, owned by Hooper's. The National Provincial Bank building, now the offices of the Halifax Building Society, was built on the site previously occupied by the premises of Masons the Chichester printers and publishers in the nineteenth century and, before that appropriately enough, the birthplace of William Collins, the poet.

▶ Jacob's Library, 25, North Street was both a newspaper shop and lending library, the original owner Mr Harry Jacobs was a bookbinder who shared the premises with his daughter, a dressmaker. It was owned later by a Mr Tielens, the books on the upper shelves of the window, innocuous by today's standards, were of great interest to the boys of the City. It closed, after 40 years in business, in 1963. This picture was taken by Leslie Holden on the day it last traded, the site is now occupied by Halfords.

Westgate, Chichester

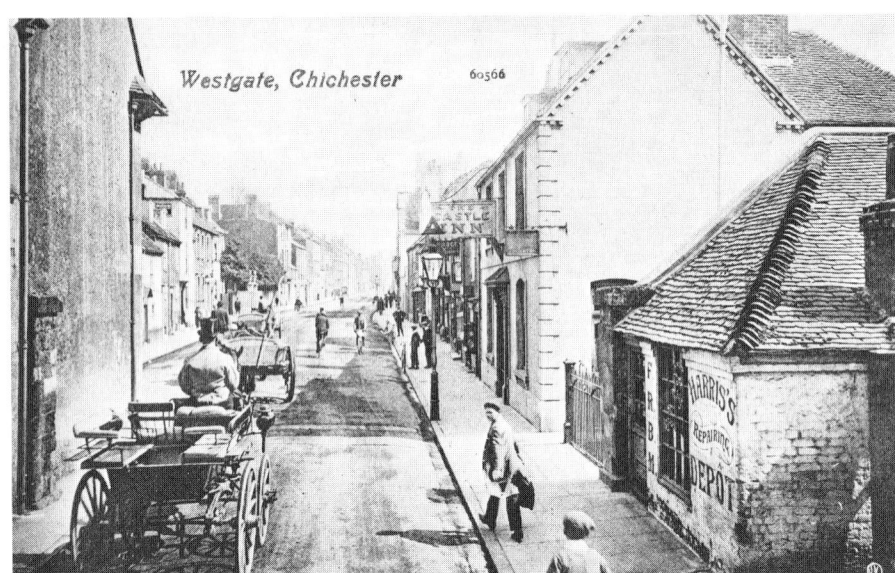

Across the road from Hopkins was Charlie Hooker's confectionery shop, I am sure many remember him as a man of military bearing with a waxed moustache that would have done a sergeant-major proud. I also include an earlier picture of the same premises taken in 1910, the building is now an Indian restaurant. It has been popularly known as The Old Toll House for many years and I do not doubt that it may have been, although I have not found any early record confirming this.

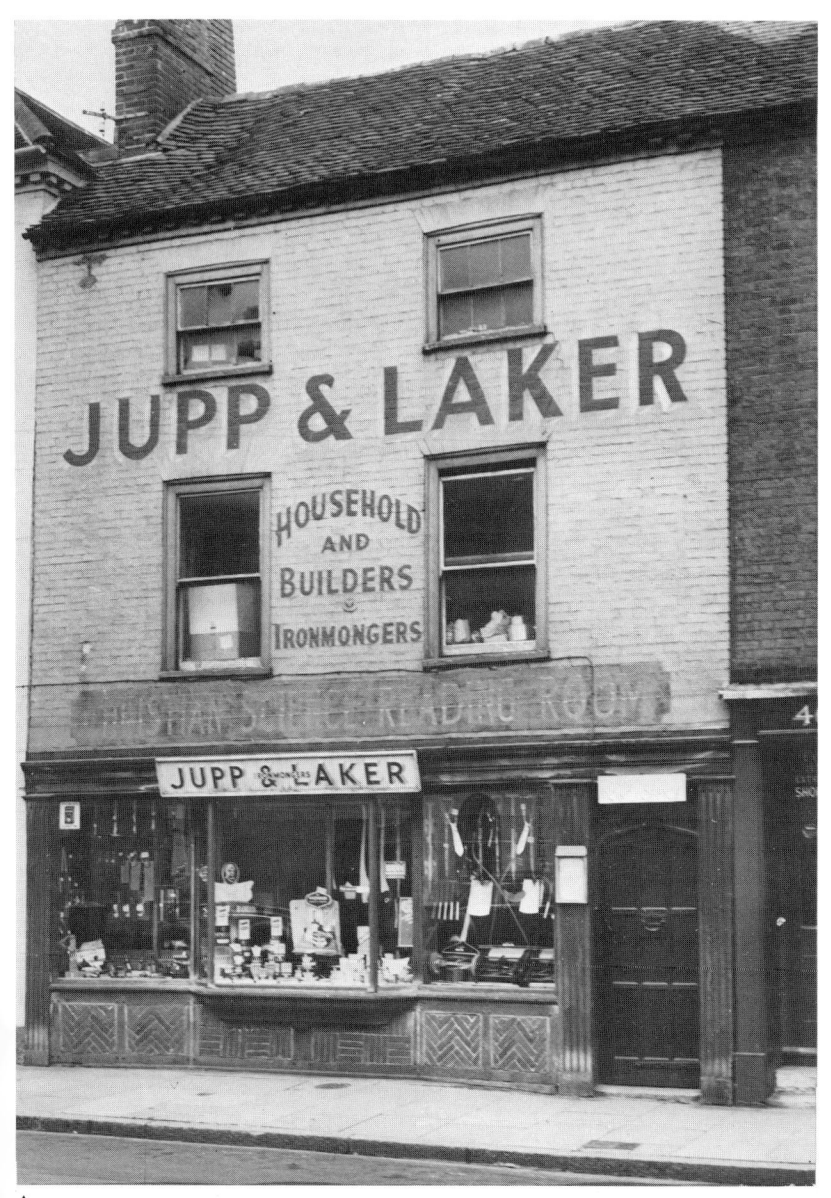

▲ Jupp and Laker's ironmongery shop. 44, North Street taken in 1951.

▲ This charming little shop, 71, North Street, was occupied by Charlie Hennings, bookmaker, for over 40 years.

11

▲ The premises featured on the right were demolished and replaced by Boots, the chemists, a 1970 picture.

▼ Turnbulls in South Street, George Turnbull was typical of the shopkeepers of the City in taking up civic duties in addition to his business interests. He served several terms as Mayor of Chichester, firstly in 1909, he was also in his time a City Alderman and a Justice of the Peace. This picture taken when the shop was up for sale in May 1963.

▼ Where were Boots before that? Just across the road next to Sykes, in those days Boots ran a lending library in addition to their pharmacy.

▲ Back to North Street, I have a Street Directory that shows that there was a fish and chip shop at No 50 as long ago as 1913, it is now Bastow's pharmacy.

The number of jeweller's shops in Chichester is a source of some amazement, obviously Cicestrians must purchase jewellery in vast quantities. It always seems to have been so, Faiths in East Street closed in 1980 but was one of the oldest, the shop having been in Faith family ownership since 1833. These pictures were lent to me by Mr A.D. Faith, great grandson of G. Faith, the founder. Among their records are the business account books of 120 years ago showing the names of many citizens who bought clocks and watches from them. In those days Faiths were also agents for the Westminster Fire Office and some of those records also survive. Mr Faith recalls tendering each year for the job of winding the Cross clock, a task he carried out many times as did his mother in the war years. Some changes had been made in the 1980 photograph. I cannot fathom out the significance of the two clocks showing different times in the earlier photograph.

▶ Next door to Faiths, (one can compare the detail on the shopfront) was Mr William Bridle a bootmaker, seen outside his shop in 1907. He must have been very proud of the impressive gas lantern over the doorway. He sold out to H & S Ford who repaired shoes here until the 1960s.

▲ Another picture taken early in the century of Smurthwaites in North Street, outside is Mr Israel Smurthwaite the founder of the firm which dealt in decorator's materials. They were taken over by Messrs Brewer & Sons who left the premises in 1988.

▲ This picture of Dunn's in South Street, now occupied by Hogg Robinson, was taken in 1910, apparently the attraction in the window was a mechanical toy model doing some knitting!

To end this series on shops here are some photographs that depict the sad sight of shops having to be shored up as the buildings had become unsafe.

In 1960 Lennards by the Cross had to be completely rebuilt and in 1969 on the other side of the Cross the building that had been Barretts the stationers and more recently had housed the Festival Theatre Offices on the ground floor suffered the same fate. In each case the structure had a timber framework dating back several centuries which by the time of these photographs could no longer support the brickwork facings imposed on them during the nineteenth century.

CHARLIE HOWARD
Sportsman, Butcher

At the corner of Green Lane and Oving Road is a buther's shop, the name on the fascia is CHARLIE HOWARD, although Charlie himself died nearly sixty years ago such was his reputation that his successors in business have retained his name ever since.

Charlie Howard was born in 1855, he was educated at the Shoreham Grammar School, he was recognised as a fine cricketer and at the age of sixteen he played for the Chichester Priory Park Cricket Club, his first game was in the match against Hastings on Tuesday September 12th 1871. He continued to play for the club for the next forty years, playing his last game at the age of 56, in the 1911 season.

He played for Sussex as a professional making his debut in 1874, of the 39 innings that he completed his highest score was 106. In 1882 he played as 12th man for the South of England Team against the Australian tourists, it is recorded that he had to sue Mr W.R. Gilbert, uncle of W.G. Grace, for his fee for playing.

Cricket was not the only game that Charlie Howard excelled at, he captained the City's teams at both Rugby and Association Football, he was also reputed to be an excellent marksman.

Charlie took over his father's business as a butcher at No 81, North Street, he was always proud of the quality of his Southdown beef, he could be seen bidding for the best cattle at Chichester Market. He was awarded a Royal Warrant in 1910 as a purveyor of meat to his Majesty King Edward VII. Thereafter a large Royal Coat of Arms was displayed over the door of his shop. (30)

In 1920 Charlie Howard bought a mare known as Chatham II for £175, he had her covered by Rock Savage, a selling plater of little success. The resulting foal, a colt was kept in a field at Fishbourne. When Charlie sensed that it might have some racing ability he named it Priory Park, after the scene of his former sporting triumphs, and sent it to be trained by George Clancy, the Lavant trainer.

Priory Park won its first race the Moulescombe Stakes at Goodwood in 1924, to celebrate this success Charlie paraded the horse around the park, it was on the 21st August 1924, the cricket team had just been trounced by Streatham, the City Band was in attendance and many citizens, quite a few of whom had won money on the race, turned out. The photograph (which appears to be a collage of two separate pictures) of Charlie with Priory Park was taken by Mr Harry Kimbell whose neice, Mrs Jenny Pine, lent it to me.

At the end of the 1924 season George Clancy left Lavant, Charlie decided to train Priory Park himself at Fishbourne, it ran unplaced in the Derby of 1925 and came third in the Royal Hunt Cup at Ascot. At Goodwood, despite having champion jockey Steve Donoghue in the saddle, it was unplaced in the Stewards Cup.

Charlie built up a string of half a dozen racehorses, including one he called 'Chichester Cross', however in 1926 he decided that at 71 he was too old to do justice to Priory Park and he reluctantly sold it to the well known racehorse owner Mr J.B. Joel for 3000 guineas. It won the 1926 Lincolnshire Handicap, starting at 20/1, then the City and Suburban Handicap and then that year's Royal Hunt Cup. In 1927 it returned to Goodwood and this time won the Stewards Cup, backed by a large proportion of the City's population, sadly it was in the colours of Mr Joel and not the primrose with Gordon tartan sash of Charlie Howard.

Between the years 1916 and 1929 Charlie Howard was the President of the Chichester City Club, he was a great benefactor of the Club, he presented a trophy for a bowling match between the City Club and teams from the Priory Park and West Sussex Clubs. He presented clocks as prizes in the annual billiards competition and he bought the cottages adjoining the Club's premises in North Pallant that a billiard room could be built at the rear of the Club, he was given the freedom of the Club in 1921.

Charlie Howard died in June 1929, he had sold his business the year before, his funeral was probably the best attended that the City has known this Century. Although his business changed hands several times until the premises closed in 1965 the Royal Arms continued to be displayed above the shopfront.

◀ Charlie with Priory Park in 1924, in what appears to be a photo montage bringing two of Chichesters most famous sporting personalities together.

▲ Charlie outside his shop taken in 1913.

CINEMAS

What did we do for entertainment in the days before the television and the video recorder? Of course one could stay at home and listen to the radio, but for many the highlight of the week was to visit one of the local cinemas, there one could be transported to another world. The cinema was a place for the young people of the City to meet with members of the opposite sex, the back row seats were always sought after by courting couples. With three picture palaces in Chichester there was usually at least one film to meet with one's taste. The cinema staff, usherettes and doormen, wore smart uniforms, the manager would always wear a dinner jacket and bow tie.

During the years just before and following the last war the cinemas were in their heyday, most evenings and certainly on Saturday night one would reckon to wait to get admission, often running from place to place to find the shortest queue.

▶ Chichester's first picture house was the Olympia in Northgate it opened in 1910 and ran until 1926 the building subsequently became the Southdown bus garage and is now used for storage. It is the only one of the City's Cinemas to still be capable of restoration to its former use, it would indeed be strange if changes in public taste were to result in it once again being the 'Electric Cinema'. As can be seen in the photograph Chichester also had a roller skating rink. Lined up outside the cinema are the staff, note the poster showing 'The Secret of the Underground Room'.

▲ The Corn Exchange building was erected in 1832 as a market place for local farmers, corn merchants and millers, it soon became apparent that the trading hall of the Exchange was ideal for drama productions and there are records of the Chichester Amateur Operatic Society and other organisations staging plays there. With the advent of the 'movies' in the 1920s Pooles Cinema gave evening film shows there until sometime in the 1930s when trading was transferred to the rear of the premises and the front part was converted to the Exchange Cinema, it survived until the early 1970s when it closed its doors for the last time, it has now been converted into a MacDonalds restaurant.

▲ In 1926 there was a cinema in a converted building in South Street known as the Picturedrome, in 1930 it was demolished together with Saunders ironmongery shop, and a new cinema was built named The Plaza. In 1950 this was taken over and re-named The Odeon, it closed finally in 1967 when the building was converted into a supermarket.

ADVERTISEMENTS

Sometimes, to those of us who get involved in such things, the Council's policies on advertising control seem unduly onerous. However these photographs, some taken as late as 1963, will remind us of a feature of the City that we are better without, it also gives an idea of what could return should the restrictions ever be relaxed. As items of nostalgia they are interesting, today's posters would not have the same appeal.

▼ The end of North Walls. T.C. Daniels handsome building albeit by now rather shabby, was demolished in 1951.

▲ Northgate, giving an idea of the first view that a visitor to the City might have encountered in the late 1950s, the building shown has been restored and is now Barclays Bank.

▼ Eastgate Square, on the corner of the Twitten to Whyke Lane taken in 1960.

▶ Southgate, no surface of any size seemed to be untouched by the postermen. The Bedford Hotel on the right was originally known as The Bedford Temperance Hotel. The date August 1958.

PUBLIC NOTICES.

Special Offer for Only Two Weeks.

SEVERAL NEW BUT SHOP SOILED

RADIO SETS

AT BARGAIN PRICES!

CALL NOW!

GARDINER'S 68, East St.
(Est. 1896)
CHICHESTER.

STREET SCENES

I have obtained many photographs showing various street scenes in Chichester taken over the last century or so, it is interesting to see the way the citizens dressed, their modes of transport and to compare the buildings with those of today.

▶ Eastgate Square, this is one of the earliest photographs of the City, it shows Market Day before the building of the Cattle Market. To help date it we can do some detective work. The Cattle Market opened in 1871, but it must have been after 1866 when the rebuilding of the spire was completed following its fall in 1861. The capstone was placed on the spire in June 1866 and the top seems to be without a weathercock, the chestnut on the left is in leaf so my estimate is about May 1866. Note the railings to the pavements, very necessary for the safety of pedestrians, compare also the shopfront of Garlands with the earlier picture shown.

▲ A view of North Street on August 31st 1946, confirming that British summers have changed little over the years. The war had not been over for a year, the lorries have only one headlight, a relic of black out restrictions.

▲ Another pre-pedestrianisation scene, this time showing Christmas shopping in East Street 1953.

▶ The Circus comes to town, Eastgate Square about 1908.

◀ Further up East Street also in 1907, see how the City's tradesmen have responded to the challenge of the automobile.

▼ East Street from a postcard dated 1907, car registration A708 stands outside Lewis the jewellers and a sign over the next shop pronounces Guy Reynolds as being 'The City Hatter'.

◀ A picture of South Street dressed for Gala Week in the early 1960s. The patchwork effect of the surfaces of the main streets is a common feature in photos of this time, it seems that, much like today they were always being dug up!

▼ A picture of West Street taken from the Bell Tower about 1920, County Hall and the Parklands Estate had not yet been built, the high buildings in the background are Westgate Brewery.

▲ Another rooftop shot, of East Street taken from the Cross in about 1900, only horse drawn traffic to be seen.

GARAGES

Some of the earlier photographs have shown the initial effect of motor cars on the street scene. In common with most towns and villages the coming of the car influenced more change in Chichester during the past Century than any other single factor.

There was an immediate decline in the number of livery stables, most of the City's inns had offered stabling and some, such as the Nags Head in St Pancras, had smithies to the rear of their premises.

It was not long before businesses sprang up to serve the motorist. Although it may seem strange today in our pedestrianised City, there were garages and petrol filling stations in all of the main streets until the 1970s, just a few of them are shown here.

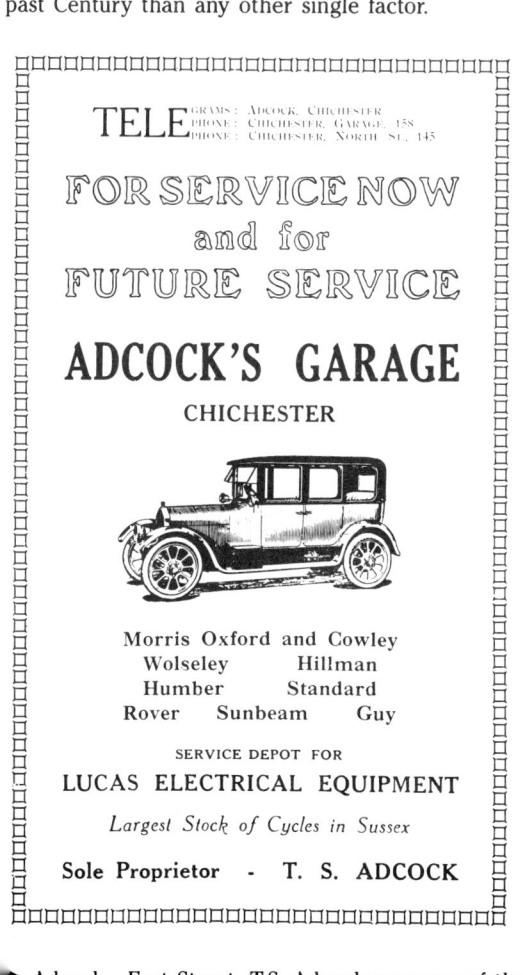

TELEGRAMS: ADCOCK, CHICHESTER
PHONE: CHICHESTER, GARAGE, 158
PHONE: CHICHESTER, NORTH ST, 145

FOR SERVICE NOW and for FUTURE SERVICE

ADCOCK'S GARAGE
CHICHESTER

Morris Oxford and Cowley
Wolseley   Hillman
Humber   Standard
Rover   Sunbeam   Guy

SERVICE DEPOT FOR
LUCAS ELECTRICAL EQUIPMENT

Largest Stock of Cycles in Sussex

Sole Proprietor - T. S. ADCOCK

Adcocks
GARAGES LIMITED
CHICHESTER
SHOWROOMS: PETROL: OFFICES
EAST STREET PHONE 2415/7 & 85402
WORKS: STORES
TERMINUS ROAD PHONE 2415/7
NIGHT BREAKDOWN SERVICE - CHI 4850
SELF DRIVE HIRE CARS

HUMBER, HILLMAN, SUNBEAM, SINGER CARS
COMMER COMMERCIAL VEHICLES
Rootes Main Dealers

▶ Adcocks, East Street. T.S. Adcock was one of the first to establish a 'motor works' in the City, he opened his premises in East Street before the First World War. He became the local dealer for Hillman and Humber cars. The company moved to the industrial estate in Terminus Road in the 1970s.

Adcock's Garages, Ltd.
(NEXT TO THIS THEATRE)

AUTOMOBILE ENGINEERS & AGENTS.

TEL. 158.   'GRAMS—Adocar.

A.A. & M.U. Agents.

Official Repairers, &c. R.A.C.

Deferred Terms.

C.A.V. Service.

Battries Charged.

Any make of Car supplied.   HIGHEST PRICE GIVEN.

DAY AND NIGHT GARAGE.

▲ Wadhams, Southgate. Wadham Brothers were the dealers for Standard cars, this picture was taken in 1959, the car outside is a 1933 Standard 'Little Nine' saloon. Now known as Wadham Stringer the successors to the business are based in Terminus Road.

▶ Fields, South Street. Fields were an old established Chichester family who transferred from hiring out horse drawn carriages to providing cars for funerals and weddings. They were the City's Austin dealers, their premises were previously occupied by Chitty's the mineral water manufacturers, in this picture, taken in 1952, we can also see the Congregational Church, since demolished.

▲ Reed's Garages. In the early 1920's Tom Reed started a car hire and taxi business from his home in Orchard Street, he went on to open these premises in West Street and later bought a second business in Northgate. The photograph was lent to me by Mrs Briant, Tom Reed's daughter.

▲ E. Allman & Co. Mrs Mollie Bowers brought me this post card, dated 1931, showing her father, John Allman, outside his garage in The Hornet, it had been built by local builder Teddy Wellcome, for a Robert Reed, who as his wife was Scots called it the Thistle Garage.

A BIG THING ACHIEVED BY STANDARD

Imagine the attractive element in cars and motoring specialised — and you will prepare yourself to meet the Standard "Big Twelve." Consider! A 13.5 h.p. six-cylinder engine developing 32.5 b.h.p. (tax £14) — for great power, fascinating speed, Four-speed, silent third gear-box — for magic management. Abundant accommodation for four passengers — yet slim, steam-lining coachwork of gallant lines. A powerful car — at an enigmatic low price! It is the production of experts who are uniquely in touch with the car-buying public's mood, needs, and spending powers. The latest model of a sensationally successful firm.

THE 1933 STANDARD "BIG TWELVE" six-cyl. Saloon **£215**. Special Saloon **£235** Two or Four seater Tourer **£215**. (Self change pre-selective gear models from **£240**.)

Also: the new Standard "Little Twelve" six-cylinder Saloon **£189**. The 1933 Standard "Little Nine" four-cylinder Saloon **£159**. The 1933 Standard "Big Nine" four-cylinder Saloon **£205**. (Self change pre-selective gear models from **£230**.) The 1933 Standard "Sixteen" six-cylinder Saloon **£235**. The 1933 Standard "Twenty" six-cylinder Saloon **£325**.

Dunlop tyres. All prices ex works.

1933 STANDARD "BIG 12"

FOR IMMEDIATE DELIVERY—

WADHAM Bros.,

SOLE DISTRICT DISTRIBUTORS:

Head Office— Waterlooville, PHONE 51.

SOUTHGATE, CHICHESTER. PHONE 182.

Also at Southampton and Southsea.

FRS. 215.

▲ Northgate Garage owned at the time of this 1958 picture by Harry Ware and later by William Pope, one time Mayor of the City.

◀ Masons Garage, Soughgate. Masons were one of the last garages to go from the main streets. Masons sold Vauxhalls and Bedford Trucks. The site is now occupied by the Waitrose Supermarket.

THE ITALIAN ICE CREAM MAN

In the foothills that lay to the South of Naples there was at the turn of the present century a small village known as Senerchia, sadly it is no more. But it was from this village that a 36 year old Italian, Emidio Guarnaccio, set forth in 1905 to try to find prosperity elsewhere. It was a time when many young Italians were leaving their country, some of Emidio's cousins had already emigrated to America. Emidio however was engaged to Petromilla Mourauda a girl from the village, he decided therefore not to go so far afield, that he could return to fetch her once he had established himself in a new country.

Emidio's travels brought him to England where he had several jobs in the southern counties, he decided that this was the country where he wished to settle. As he had promised, he went back to Senerchia, married Petromilla and returned with her to set up home. At first they worked and lived in various places in the Redhill and Reigate area of Surrey, they entered the licensed trade becoming landlords of a pub in Petersfield, by this time they had three sons Michael, Peter and John. They suspected that the pub was haunted, John clearly remembered for the rest of his life, seeing a man's figure standing at the foot of his bed each night. They quickly moved to Havant where they took over the 'Old House at Home'.

In 1920 they were able to purchase a grocery and general stores shop in Northgate, Chichester. They lived over the premises. At the rear there were some lodging rooms, known locally, rather impolitely, as the 'Doss House', customers, who were mostly vagrants, would be charged one penny for a nights bed.

Emidio started to manufacture ice cream, a product that Italians were noted for, he became a well known sight as he trundled his 'Stop Me and Buy One' barrow around the City's parks and streets. In 1929 he and Petromilla had a new house built for them in Whyke Road. By now Michael and John were helping them in the business. The manufacture of their ice cream took place in a building at the rear of their house, and in the summer months Emidio and John's day would start at 4am when they would make their ice cream, Emidio would load the barrow and push it all the way to Selsey to sell his ices on Selsey beach. If the weather was good then, at midday, John would follow in a Morris van to meet his father by the Albion Pub with a further supply. The family's day would end about 10pm with the cleaning of their equipment ready for the next day's trading. In later years when the Selsey Tram train service had a luggage truck they would use that to transport the barrow.

The business in Northgate was sold in 1929, when the new house was built, and in 1933 Michael opened a similar shop opposite the old premises in North Street, called 'Mickey's', the name by which he was known to all. He soon became established as one of the City's true characters, his shop was open from seven in the morning to ten at night, every day of the week including Sundays. Mickey was always to be found wearing a waistcoat and a cap and usually with a cigarette hanging from his lips and using one of his scale weights as an ashtray. He would often give credit to the nurses at the local hospitals, by quite literally keeping a slate with the debt of each, mostly for sweets and cigarettes, chalked up against settling day when they received their monthly pay packets.

Although not generally known at the time Mickey made a generous gift to the Royal West Sussex Hospital, enabling cot sides to be provided in the geriatric wards.

Emidio died, aged 96, in 1966. During the war years he had taken over the running of Mickey's shop. John's son Martin Guarnaccio still lives and works in Chichester; among the family mementoes he treasures the 'Documento di Emigrazionne' issued by the Italian authorities to his grandfather in 1905.

Guarnaccio's Shop in Northgate taken soon after they had disposed of the business.

◀ Emidio Guarnaccio selling ice cream on Selsey beach in 1928.

▼ Mickey's shop in North Street, Mickey can be seen outside.

▼ Mickey in his shop, taken in 1976.

A WALK DOWN EAST STREET

I have managed to collect enough old photographs to create a walk down the South side of East Street as it was in the 1960's. The amount of change that has taken place is surprising, alterations have taken place and shops have inevitably gone. However it has happened so gradually that until seeing a record such as this, one may not realize that although Pines and Bevis's are still in Eastgate Square, none of the shops that were on this side of East Street in 1960 have survived into 1989.

▶ Since this picture was taken the two houses on the left have had shop fronts inserted into them, both Lansley the Tailor and Howards the photographers have gone. Lansleys was a much travelled business he started in premises by the Cross in the 1920s, he moved to No 36 East Street and then to the premises shown in this picture, from here he later moved to St Johns Street.

NOTICE OF REMOVAL.

ARTHUR LANSLEY,

High-class Practical Tailor,
: Hatter and Shirt Maker :

Liveries, Mackintoshes, Uniforms   *Spécialité*: "Ready to Wear"
and Breeches.   Raincoats.
Ladies' Costumes.

HAS REMOVED from THE CROSS to
36a EAST STREET, CHICHESTER.

Telephone 30.   Tel. Add.: "Lansley, Chichester."

▼ Goodridge's Motor Cycle Shop had been in these premises since 1928, formerly the building was the City Fire Engine House. The cafe was at one time the Market Tavern.

▶ The car park next to Adcocks was the site of the Chichester Police Station demolished in 1967. I have shown a photograph of Adcocks earlier in the section on garages, this is now the site of Friar's House and the DHSS offices.

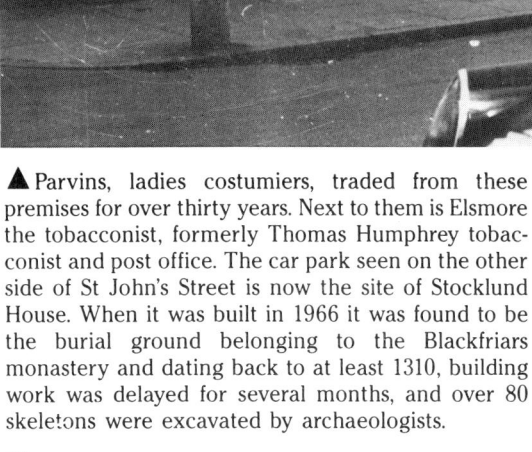

▲ Parvins, ladies costumiers, traded from these premises for over thirty years. Next to them is Elsmore the tobacconist, formerly Thomas Humphrey tobacconist and post office. The car park seen on the other side of St John's Street is now the site of Stocklund House. When it was built in 1966 it was found to be the burial ground belonging to the Blackfriars monastery and dating back to at least 1310, building work was delayed for several months, and over 80 skeletons were excavated by archaeologists.

▲ The Fleece Inn, at one time called The Golden Fleece and before that The Bell, was one of the City's oldest establishments, it was both a coaching inn and a brewery and is reputed to be the birthplace of William Cawley the Chichester MP of the 17th Century. As can be seen it was formerly much larger, taking in the building occupied at the time of this picture by Messrs Wyatt & Son, estate agents, now the Prudential. The old stable buildings are still to be seen in the yard at the rear of the pub which closed in 1988.

▶ Adams the Butcher and Gardiner's radio and cycle shop, businesses that seemed like Chichester institutions in their time. However they have both now gone, they could not compete with the large multi-shop combines.

Notice over Adam's premises, Batchelor's Registry Office for Servants, another sign of times past.

▼ The Rendezvous Cafe was one of the many tea rooms that abounded in the main streets, each had their own clientele of regulars. The Rendezvous was a favourite place for a pot of tea on a wet Sunday afternoon. Often to be seen there was Fred Bell, a well known Chichester eccentric of the years just before and after the war, reputed to be a chess genius he had books on the subject published. He often risked life and limb directing traffic in East Street, thereby perhaps freeing a 'regular' member of the Police force to consider his lot with more ease as this constable of 1959 vintage is obviously doing.

43

▼ Elphick's, a name synonomous to gourmets and to the citizens of Chichester, with Pork Sausages alas they closed in 1987 after 60 years in business. The secret of their sausages was in the way they minced their meat, eschewing modern methods, and in the spices. Fortunately the formula has been divulged by the partners to Reeds, the Kingsham butchers, who sell them in Chichester Market.

▶ I discovered this photograph in the museum archives and include it to show how little the upper floors of the building have changed since 1905. The Mr Doman in the photograph who founded the firm in 1868, was the grandfather of D.R. Doman, his father presumably being the 'son' referred to on the sign.

◀ Doman's were a part of the City business community for over a century, they had another shop in North Street.

▼ The Tudor Cafe was under the same ownership as the Tower Cafe in West Street, many Chichester couples had their wedding reception graced by a cake from the Tudor. The corner occupied by Breeches at the time of the picture was the site of the George Inn in 1623.

▲ The upper storeys of this group of shops have changed little since 1959 when this photograph was taken. However none of the businesses have survived. At the rear of Lewis's, the tobacconists, there was a barber shop run by Eddie Smith who took the business over from his father, among Eddie's customers was Bishop Bell and many other Cathedral dignatory.

◀ Many older Chichester residents will look at this photograph and the smell of Macfisheries will be remembered, it was not exactly unpleasant, but memorable nevertheless. Laceys, owned by Sydney Lacey, were stationers with branches in Bognor Regis and Worthing. The Maypole premises have suffered the same fate as many others and are now the local branch offices of a building society.

▲ Kimbell & Son were an old Chichester business that closed as long ago as 1968 having been pork butchers and bacon curers in these premises for over 50 years, this photograph taken in January 1952.

CHECK THAT COLD
WITH
"ZUBES"
FROM
WHITES
29, EAST STREET, CHICHESTER.
Stockists of "MARS."

▲ Timothy Whites, after their takeover by Boots, exchanged premises with them, moving to the shop now occupied by Comet in South Street. One doubts if the penny weighing machine would survive unvandalised on today's streets.

LAST ORDERS AT THE BAR

When William Hudson, the naturalist and travel writer, came to Chichester in the 1880s he was appalled at what he saw. It was a City that none of us would recognise today. He later wrote about a Chichester with seventy public houses, open from eight in the morning to eleven at night, and dozens of 'off' licenses and wine and spirit merchants. He saw 'utterly drink-degraded wretches' stumbling forth from the pubs and groups of intoxicated men standing about the Cross and on street corners in the mud and rain.

The number of public houses in the City has been reduced drastically since those times. In the early part of the Century the magistrates revoked many of the licenses. In more recent years lack of car parking space has proved a factor leading to the decline in popularity for some, others could not offer the bar accommodation needed to meet today's standards, and, in a few cases, the site on which they stood had development potential well in excess of their value as a public house.

Chichester, showing Roads to Arundel and Bognor.

▲ There are still Cicestrians who can remember the old Unicorn Inn in Eastgate Square, this picture was taken in 1911 when there was a water pump in the centre of the square to which had been attached signs indicating the roads to Arundel and Bognor. There is a record of a Unicorn Inn being on the same site in 1689, it is doubtful whether the building shown is the original inn, although it is thought possible that the original framework was refronted in brickwork in the intervening years.

The old building was demolished in 1935, the new Unicorn that was erected in its place was the showpiece of Messrs Henty & Constable, the Chichester brewing firm. I can remember attending a Christmas party, held there for the children of the brewery employees, in 1939. The war years were particularly active for the Unicorn which was adopted by the R.A.F. aircrews from Tangmere as their 'local'. The landlord during those years was Arthur King. The story has often been told how he was responsible for the idea of flying a barrel of Henty's Chichester Ale, slung under the wings of a Spitfire, to R.A.F. personnel in France in the latter days of the war.

The Unicorn closed as a pub in 1960 and the building became the studios for the Chichester Festival Theatre, changing its name to The Minerva Studios. In 1982 the building was reconstructed internally to provide office accommodation.

▲ This is a photograph taken outside the Crown Inn in Whyke Road in about 1890, the occasion was the change of landlord. On the right of the picture, with his children, is Mr Eyles who was taking over the house.

▶ Outside the City bounds for a photograph of The Island Cottage at North Mundham, taken about 1910.

▲ The Roundabout Inn was on the Corner of Bognor Road and Whyke Road. I am told it was a favourite haunt for Selsey Fishermen, who would bring fish to be sold in the City and on the way back call in to quench their thirst. Apparently this quenching often went on till closing time when they would return home via Hunston on foot.

▼ In this photograph of the Hornet, taken in 1911, one can only just see The Four Chesnuts but I thought it worth including to give an idea of what the Hornet looked like at that time. The pub has changed little. When I first saw the new sign I doubted whether the spelling was correct, but found that it is corroborated by the Chichester Directory of 1910.

▼ The Victoria was, I understand, converted from a large house to a brewery in about 1880. This photograph was taken at the turn of the Century when it was owned by the Constable family, later to merge with the Chichester brewing firm of Henty & Co. Interesting to see that besides supplying families they also catered for cyclists with their wines and spirits.

▲ I include this picture of the yard at Henty & Constable's Brewery in Westgate taken in 1928, my father worked here from about this time until they sold out in 1954. There had been a brewery on this site since the beginning of the nineteenth century. Note the steam drawn vehicle loading up barrels.

This picture of the Foresters Arms in North Street was taken in about 1911 when it was decorated for the Coronation. To know where this pub was compare this picture with that of Mickey's shop, I am told that Mickey's counter was once the bar.

CHURCHES

For a cathedral city Chichester has been remarkably careless with its churches, so many seem to have gone in the last fifty years. From about 1800 onwards there was a dramatic increase in the population of the City, and as a result, there was an upsurge in Church attendances, which in turn resulted in a spate of Church building for all denominations.

Most of these Churches remained in use well into the present Century, however diminishing congregations, together with the high cost of maintenance and repair, caused many to become redundant or to amalgamate with others. Those that could not be found a use for were demolished.

▶ Probably the most bizarre change of use is that of the former Primitive Methodist Church in the Hornet, built in 1865 it closed for worship in 1968, it is now a Chinese takeaway restaurant.

◀ The Congregational Church in South Street was built in 1892. In 1978 the members of the church decided to join with the Methodists and to both sell their premises so that they could unite in one new building. As a result the church shown in this photograph has now been demolished and the site re-developed for shopping use.

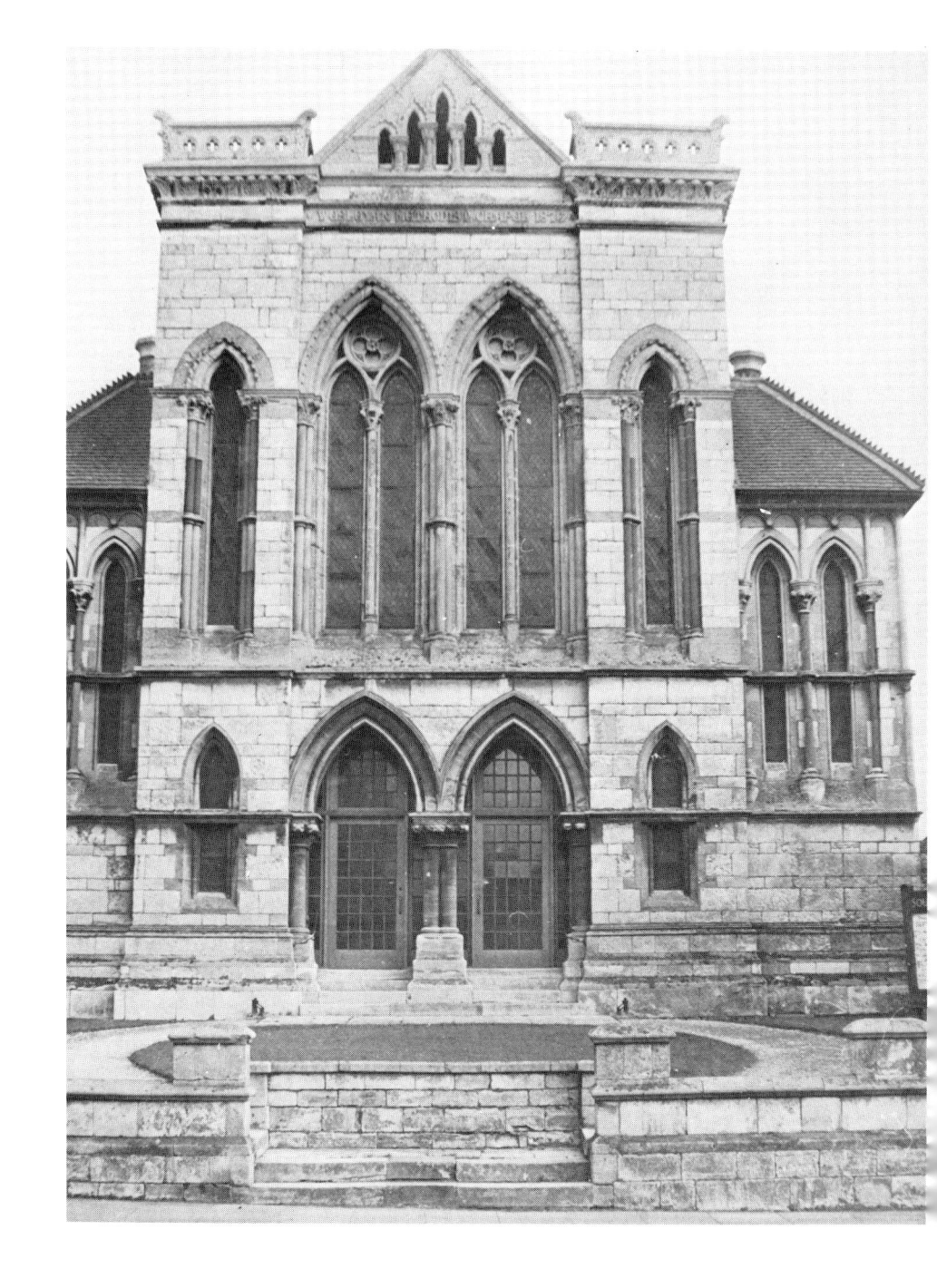

▶ Southgate Methodist Church, this fine building, which was completed in 1877 was the other partner in the arrangement involving the Congregational Church, it too was demolished to make way for shops in 1981.

▲ St Richard's Roman Catholic church was erected in 1855, it became too small to cater for the number of worshippers and was demolished and the site sold when the new St Richards was opened in Market Avenue in 1958.

◀ St Peter the Less North Street, of all of the churches shown in this section this church is the one that surely should not have been demolished. I doubt whether it would be today. Some authorities dated it back to Saxon times, making it an older building than the Cathedral, one cannot believe that the (former Co-op) building that now graces the site in any way compensates Cicestrians for the loss.

▲ For some years after the demolition this was all that remained of possibly the oldest site of Christian worship in Chichester.

THE CITY CELEBRATES

The citizens of Chichester have always been enthusiastic in celebrating royal occasions although sadly, as these pictures show, the quality of the street decorations has declined somewhat over the years.

The Golden and Diamond Jubilees of Queen Victoria's Reign in 1887 and 1897 were celebrated throughout Britain and the Empire. In Chichester the festivities included a luncheon at the Corn Exchange, processions, athletics, firework displays, bonfires and the erection of decorated arches on the original sites of the four city gates.

▲ Eastgate 1897.

An impressive gate which seems to obstruct the doors of the city fire station. The bells at the top of the picture are those of the old City Police Station.

59

▲ North Street 1897.
The Jubilee Parade seems to have more participants than spectators.

▲ This is the only photograph that I have been able to find of the 1902 Coronation of Edward VII, the unusual pump and street light in the centre of Eastgate Square was reputedly made in one casting by Halsteds, the Chichester Ironfounders.

▲ The City celebrated again in 1911 for the Coronation of George V. This time the workmanship put into building the facsimile gates was remarkable, each gate was the responsibility of a group of the City's tradesmen, the teams vied with each other to produce the most outstanding design, this was Northgate. The shop on the left obscured by the 'gate' was A.E. Osborn, Fruiterer and later T.C. Daniels. On the right was E.K. Turbin, then later Guarnaccio and then Briants, the shop was demolished in 1953.

▲ Southgate 1911.
A fine photograph taken by Russells the Chichester photographer, on the right the Roman Catholic church of St Richard and on the left an attractive lady at the door of The Fountain. Russell's the photographers were apparently 'under Royal Patronage', from the quality of this series of three studies it is easy to see why.

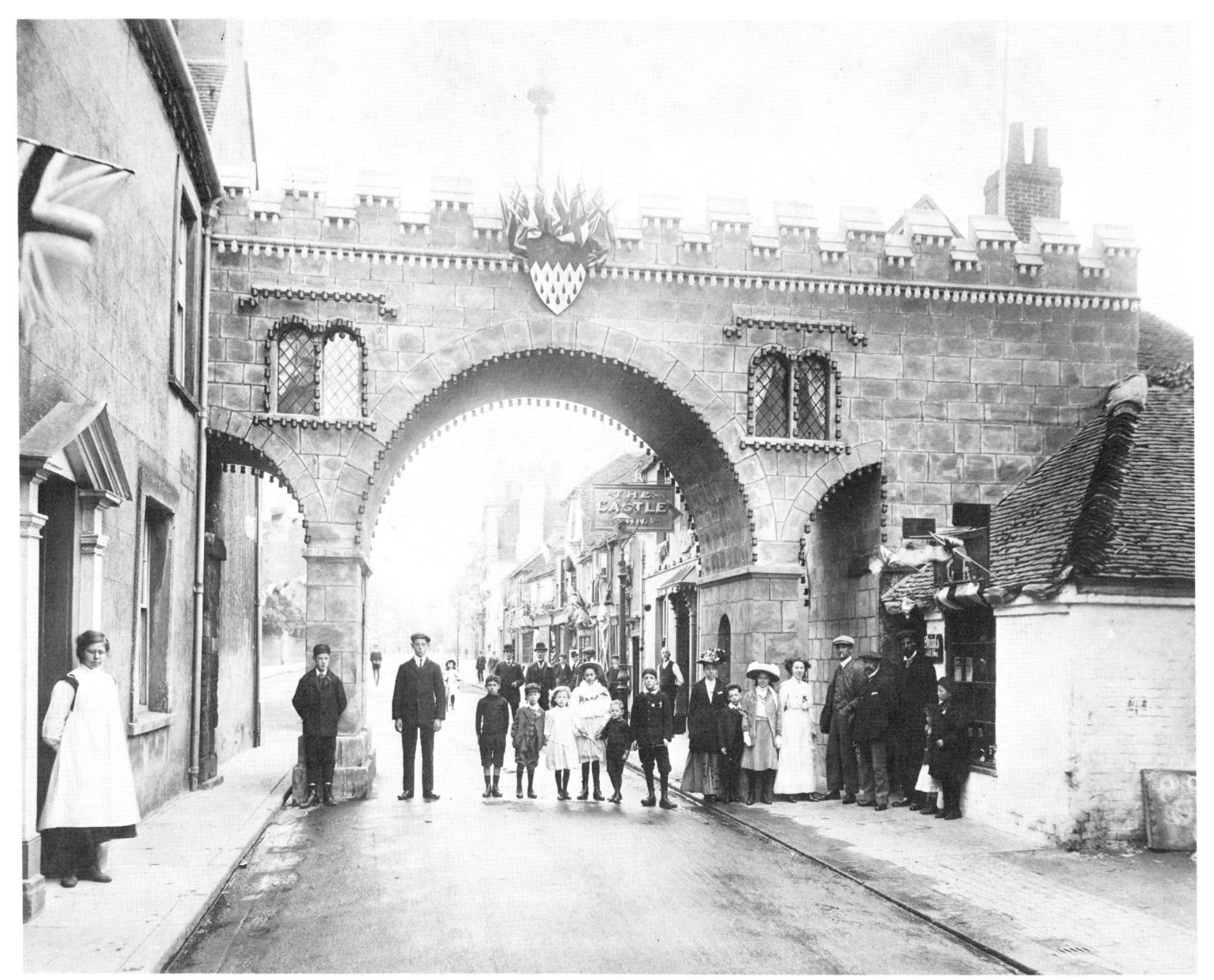

▲Westgate 1911.

This picture can be compared with the one shown earlier in the book another young lady at a doorway, this time at No 4. Westgate, home at that time of Alderman John Holt, J.P., City Mayor in 1907 and 1908. The young lady may have been his daughter.

▲ Eastgate 1911.
Note the lad perched precariously on the top of this 'ruined' arch, also the Market Tavern on the left.

▲ For the coronation of George VI in 1937 the streets were decorated with flags and bunting as this picture of Eastgate shows.

▲ There was also a competition for the best decorated house, here is the winning house in St Pancras owned by a Mr Brookes.

Finally and almost apologetically some photographs of Chichester streets decorated in June 1953 for the Coronation of Queen Elizabeth II.

▲ North Street.

▲ East Street.

▶ South Street taken through the Cross. Perhaps the Queen's Golden Jubilee in 2003 will be celebrated with something to rival the efforts of our predecessors, it would be highly appropriate if this book whose cover displays several of these gates were to prompt the formation of new groupings of the City's traders to start planning now for that occasion.

69

CHICHESTER'S POSTAL PAST

I am told that there are many enthusiasts who research postal history. I hope they and others enjoy the following photographs.

Some of the postmen outside the building on the day that Chichester's first petrol driven vehicle arrived, note the proud driver in his leather greatcoat.

▲ An early photograph showing the delivery men about to set off on their rounds by horse and cart, handcart and bicycle.

▶ The interior of the Chichester sorting office 1912.

A remarkable series of badly faded photographs showing the funeral in 1907 of John Little the Chichester Postmaster setting out from the Post Office. He was the first, full time, salaried Postmaster for Chichester and lived on the premises. I make no apologies for including these poorly reproduced photographs, I felt the interesting subject matter outweighed the quality requirement.

▲ First the undertaker leading the cortege of six carriages.

▶ The last carriage is followed by the walking mourners.

72

◄ To become a postman it was necessary to have served one's time as a telegraph boy, here they can be seen following up the procession. It is interesting to note that as the procession goes out of view how the people who have been watching it pass, return to their daily tasks.

▼ The South Street building in 1960 when it was in use only as the sorting office.

TREASURE TROVE

Many people, knowing of my interest in Chichester, have been kind enough to lend me photographs that they have had tucked away for years. I almost have enough to provide another volume. I conclude with a selection of some of the most interesting.

It may seem surprising to younger readers that horse drawn deliveries of milk, coal, beer and other commodities were quite commonplace until relatively recent times.

▼ You see here my father-in-law, Dick Weston, who delivered milk in the City for over fifty years. During the war, when on leave from the Army, he always made a point of visiting his horse, Kit. Dick tells the story of the day when Kit disgraced herself by bolting from North Street and up College Lane finally being found in fields at Graylingwell, only the shafts of the cart remained, the rest 'smashed like matchwood' was strewn along the route of her flight.

◀ The Easter meeting of Lord Gifford's Hounds at Fishbourne in 1911, I have identified the house on the left as being No 104 Fishbourne Road. Lord Gifford, who lived at Old Park, Bosham, obtained a High Court injunction against the Chichester Corporation in 1904 to stop the sewage works creating an unpleasant odour that apparently travelled to his property.

▼ A photograph taken in the early years of the Second War when Greyfriars, the City Council offices in North Street, were partly taken over as the headquarters of the local Civil Defence operation.

▲ A mystery photograph. If any reader is able to enlighten me I would be interested to know. Titled 'Drawing Lord Edmund Talbot's Car through Chichester'. It is worth including if only to show the buildings in the background, one can see the old police station, centre left. Mrs Alice Brazier's fishmongery became a fried fish shop in about 1925, later on her daughters re-opened the shop as a wool shop.

▲ This is a very sad photograph of Southgate. All of the buildings shown were demolished to make way for the Avenue De Chartres.

▲ I have already mentioned Tom Reed who owned Garages in West Street and Northgate, he started in business by hiring cars, here are four of them, Model 'T' Fords I believe, dressed for a wedding but waiting outside the gates to the Cattle Market in 1923!

▶ Shambles Alley which is now the footpath from North Street, alongside Macari's, to St Martins Street. It was largely demolished by bombs in the War and then finished off by the City Council afterwards to give rear access and parking for the Buttermarket.

I find photographs of groups of people fascinating, it is always interesting trying to find out the names of as many as possible, I am sure readers who have lived in the City will spot some they know in the later pictures.

▲ The staff of Shippams outside their shop in South Street, now Millets.

▲ George Gilbert performed a great service to the young men of Chichester when he founded the Gilbertians Cricket Club in 1949, it is now forty years old and George is the club's president. This photograph shows the 1953 team, George is on the left, the umpire is Charlie Newell.

CHICHESTER CITY GUARD. AT DRILL. MOREY. ST PANCRAS STUDIO. 10. CHI

It seems there is little solid information available on the Chichester City Guard. Here they are whoever they may be and whatever their purpose, on manoeuvres. We do know the hatless man, he is Arthur ...ley, the photograph was taken in Priory Park about ...12.

▲ Girls and boys of the High Schools also in Priory Park, this was for Empire Day 1930, the teacher is Miss Richards.

▲ Another school portrait, this one of a class in the Central Girls School in Chapel Street in 1931, the picture was lent to me by Mrs Patterson who, as Freda White, is nearest the camera.

▲ The Bishop Otter College trained many young ladies to become school teachers, in 1989 it celebrated the centenary of its re-formation as a ladies college, it was originally a men's college. This picture shows the residents of 'Long Dormitory' in 1911.

Adcock's Garages, Ltd.

(NEXT TO THIS THEATRE).

AUTOMOBILE ENGINEERS & AGENTS.

TEL. 158.

A.A. & M.U. Agents.

Official Repairers, &c. R.A.C.

'GRAMS—Adocar.

Deferred Terms.

C.A.V. Service.

Batteries Charged.

Any make of Car supplied.   HIGHEST PRICE GIVEN.

DAY AND NIGHT GARAGE.

Adcocks
GARAGES LIMITED
CHICHESTER

SHOWROOMS: PETROL: OFFICES
EAST STREET   PHONE 2415/7 & 85402

WORKS: STORES
TERMINUS ROAD   PHONE 2415/7

NIGHT BREAKDOWN SERVICE - CHI 4850

SELF DRIVE HIRE CARS

HUMBER, HILLMAN, SUNBEAM, SINGER CARS

COMMER COMMERCIAL VEHICLES

Rootes Main Dealers

BE SURE YOUR CAR IS MADE IN THE UNITED KINGDOM

FIRST APPEARANCE

AUSTIN's
NEW SIX-WINDOW TEN-FOUR
The Sherborne £178

The Sherborne Fixed-Head Saloon £162. 10s.

Here's a new family saloon with every up-to-the-minute luxury in equipment and finish. Comfort in the way of head, leg and elbow room has been specially considered in this new model. Its flexible engine develops unusual power and is mounted on the dependable Austin Ten-Four chassis which has proved so highly efficient and immensely popular. May we give you fuller particulars of the new six-window Sherborne?

THE AUSTIN SHERBORNE HAS: Downswept, flush back-panel enclosing spare wheel and luggage carrier; six wide side-windows; deeply-valanced, wide mudwings; anatomically correct seating; hour-glass steering; fool-proof controls; exceptional stability and safety through low centre of gravity, and smooth, powerful brakes.

The Lichfield models, as a result of economies in manufacture, have been reduced in price, as follows: Lichfield 4-window Saloon £168. Lichfield Fixed-Head Saloon £152.10s. Prices at works—effective from January 24th.

READ THE AUSTIN MAGAZINE: FOURPENCE EVERY MONTH.

Adcock's Garages Ltd.
EAST STREET ———— CHICHESTER

YOU BUY A CAR — BUT YOU INVEST IN AN AUSTIN

TELE GRAMS: Adcock, Chichester
PHONE: Chichester, Garage, 158
PHONE: Chichester, North St., 145

FOR SERVICE NOW and for FUTURE SERVICE

ADCOCK'S GARAGE

CHICHESTER

Morris Oxford and Cowley
Wolseley   Hillman
Humber   Standard
Rover   Sunbeam   Guy

SERVICE DEPOT FOR

LUCAS ELECTRICAL EQUIPMENT

Largest Stock of Cycles in Sussex

Sole Proprietor - T. S. ADCOCK

A BIG THING ACHIEVED BY STANDARD

Imagine the attractive element in cars and motoring specialised — and you will prepare yourself to meet the Standard "Big Twelve." Consider ! A 13.5 h.p. six-cylinder engine developing 32.5 b.h.p. (tax £14) — for great power, fascinating speed, Four-speed, silent third gear-box — for magic management. Abundant accommodation for four passengers — yet slim, steam-lining coachwork of gallant lines. A powerful car — at an enigmatic low price ! It is the production of experts who are uniquely in touch with the car-buying public's mood, needs, and spending powers. The latest model of a sensationally successful firm.

THE 1933 STANDARD "BIG TWELVE" six-cyl. Saloon £215. Special Saloon £235 Two or Four seater Tourer £215. (*Self change pre-selective gear models from £240.*)

Also: the new Standard "Little Twelve" six-cylinder Saloon £189. The 1933 Standard "Little Nine" four-cylinder Saloon £159. The 1933 Standard "Big Nine" four-cylinder Saloon £205. (*Self change pre-selective gear models from £230*). The 1933 Standard "Sixteen" six-cylinder Saloon £235. The 1933 Standard "Twenty" six-cylinder Saloon £325.

Dunlop tyres. All prices ex works.

1933 STANDARD "BIG 12"

FOR IMMEDIATE DELIVERY—

WADHAM Bros.,

SOLE DISTRICT DISTRIBUTORS:

Head Office—   **SOUTHGATE,**   Also at Southampton
Waterlooville.   **CHICHESTER.**   and Southsea.
PHONE 51.   PHONE 182.

FRS. 215.

WILLIAM FARR   REMOVAL & CARTAGE CONTRACTOR CHICHESTER
COAL AND COKE MERCHANT
ESTABLISHED 1850

PUBLIC NOTICES.

Special Offer for Only Two Weeks.

SEVERAL NEW BUT SHOP SOILED

RADIO SETS

AT BARGAIN PRICES!

CALL NOW!

GARDINER'S 68, East St.
(Est. 1896)
CHICHESTER.

HEINZ
P
DOGS
If you knows of a better beer, drink it!
FRIARY ALES
OXO
MAKES COOKING SO EASY
Surf
LATHERS LIKE MAGIC!
FIRST EVER TO GIVE YOU both the cleanest wash and the whitest boil!

GARDEN TOOLS & REQUISITES

E. F. SAUNDERS
55, South Street, CHICHESTER

The recognised Establishment for best value in Household Ironmongery, Garden Tools and Sporting Requisites, Tools for the Home, Workshop and Garden.

CYCLE.   ELECTRIC LAMPS.
ACCESSORIES.   BELLS & REFILLS.

Fishing Tackle. Guns and Ammunition.
Cutlery. ∴ Gas Lamps and Fittings.

NEXT SHOP TO G.P.O.

Razors, Scissors and Cutlery ground on premises. Safety Razor Blades re-sharpened on premises by Electrical Machinery.

TENANT OF THE ANCIENT CRYPT (see page 19) WHICH MAY BE INSPECTED BY CUSTOMERS.

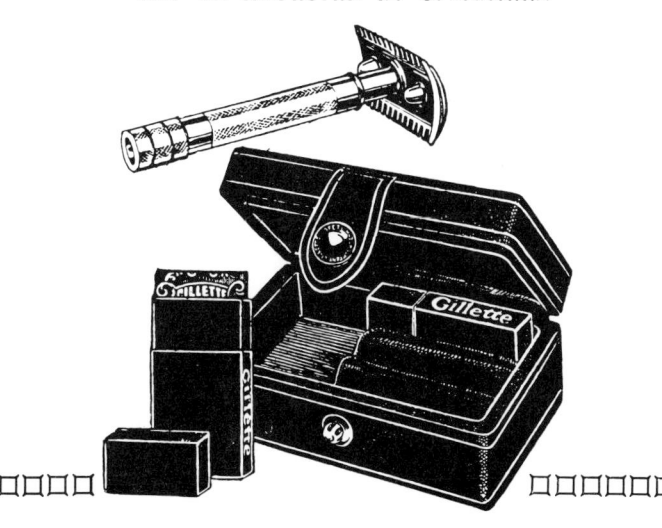

CHARLIE HOWARD
FAMILY BUTCHER

Purveyor to the late King

Home-killed English Meat only

FAMILIES WAITED UPON DAILY FOR ORDERS

Specialities:
Prime Ox Beef & Southdown Mutton
NORTH STREET, CHICHESTER

Telephone, 167 Chichester.   Telephone, 121 Bognor.

KIMBELL & SONS

ESTABLISHED OVER **60** YEARS.

| ENGLISH CHEDDARS —and— STILTONS For Christmas. | **PORK BUTCHERS,** Bacon & Ham Curers, and Provision Merchants. | ENGLISH HAMS —and— BACONS For Chr stmas. |

Manufacturers of the CELEBRATED SUSSEX SAUSAGES.

Manufactory—CHICHESTER.

4, London Road, BOGNOR.

HAMS COOKED : : FREE : : *By the Latest Methods*

87, East Street, CHICHESTER.

Telephone No. 97

SIDNEY BASTOW

PHARMACEUTICAL CHEMIST & OPTICIAN

(By Examination)

PRESCRIPTIONS DISPENSED

Sole Proprietor of THORP'S BALSAMIC COUGH MIXTURE & THORP'S CHICHESTER LIVER PILLS

All KODAK SUPPLIES

DARK ROOM

ALL MAKES OF PLATES, FILMS AND PAPER. DEVELOPING AND PRINTING

A 24 HOUR SERVICE

9 North Street, Chichester

FACING TECHNICAL INSTITUTE

SPIRELLA CORSETS

These Famous Corsets are unrivalled for Style, Comfort and Health, and have a perfectly Flexible and Unbreakable Boning, which always keeps its shape no matter how long the garment is worn. All types of figures suited. Maternity Corsets a speciality. Very lightly boned Corsets for growing girls: give good poise and easy carriage of figure. Cleaning and Repairing done.

THE MISSES GORHAM

Specialists in Corrective Corsetry

13 ST. MARTIN'S ST., CHICHESTER

Representatives also for Bognor, Selsey and surrounding districts, visit Bognor on Tuesdays and Fridays. Appointments made for fitting and adjustment.

Telegrams—SELSEY HOTEL, Selsey. Phone **17** SELSEY.

SELSEY HOTEL
SELSEY-ON-SEA.

Officially appointed by the R.A.C. & A.A., and nearest Hotel to Station and Golf Links.

Tennis Courts and Bowling Green in own ground.

LARGE GARAGE. : CARS FOR HIRE.

GOOD ENGLISH CATERING.

TARIFF ON APPLICATION

Proprietor - G. ROWLAND.

NOTICE OF REMOVAL.

ARTHUR LANSLEY,

High-class Practical Tailor,
: Hatter and Shirt Maker :

Liveries, Mackintoshes, Uniforms and Breeches.

Spécialité : "Ready to Wear" Raincoats.

Ladies' Costumes.

HAS REMOVED from THE CROSS to

36a EAST STREET, CHICHESTER.

Telephone 30.   Tel. Add.: "Lansley, Chichester."

SPECIALITIES FOR INVALIDS.

SHARP GARLAND

Offers the following suggestions to those who require a Tonic or "Pick-me-Up" to restore them to health after the ravages of Influenza and other winter ailments. First and foremost try—

GILBEY'S celebrated **INVALID PORT** ... at 4/6 per bot. 2/6 per ½ bot.
specially selected **INVALID CHAMPAGNE** in ¼ bot. 2/9. ½ bot. 4/6.
VIBRONA, the ideal Tonic Wine ... ... 6/- per bot.
WINCARNIS and **HALL'S WINE** ... ... 3/3 and 5/6 per bot.
EMU TONIC WINE (Australian) ... ... 3/- and 5/- per bot.
BRAND'S BEEF and **CHICKEN ESSENCES** and **JELLIES, LUSTY'S REAL TURTLE SOUP, VALENTINE'S MEAT JUICE,** Etc.

The EASTGATE STORES, CHICHESTER.

Established 1665.   Telephone 89.

Full Head £2.

Sides only £1.

THE NEW **NON-ELECTRICAL**
Permanent Wave.

"Sartory" Safety System.

Steaming instead of Baking at

RANDS,
75, EAST STREET, CHICHESTER.
Phone 43.

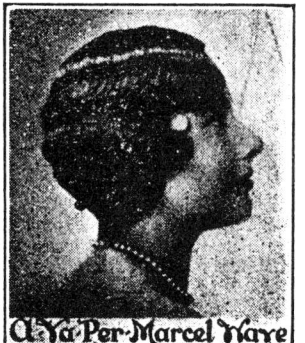

A Ya-Per-Marcel Wave

PHONE 407
EXCHANGE
CHICHESTER.

TO-DAY AND ALL THIS WEEK.

IVOR NOVELLO,
ELIZABETH ALLAN — A. W. BASKCOMB

"THE LODGER"
Britain's Best Thriller!

Also "The Clock Store," Silly Symphony Cartoon.

NEXT MONDAY, TUESDAY & WEDNESDAY
(January 23rd, 24th and 25th).

WINIFRED SHOTTER
AND
OWEN NARES
IN
THE LOVE CONTRACT

The fascinating Musical Romance in which Winifred Shotter amazed the British Film Industry, and became a "Star."

CHECK THAT COLD
WITH
"ZUBES"
FROM
WHITES
29, EAST STREET, CHICHESTER.

Stockists of "MARS."

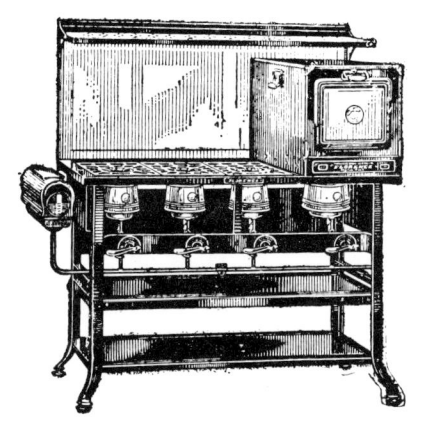

Florence Oil Cookers.

Silence.
No Smoke. No Smell.
No Pumping. No Wick.

HALSTED & SONS,
The City Ironmongers, LTD.,
Chichester.

The PLAZA

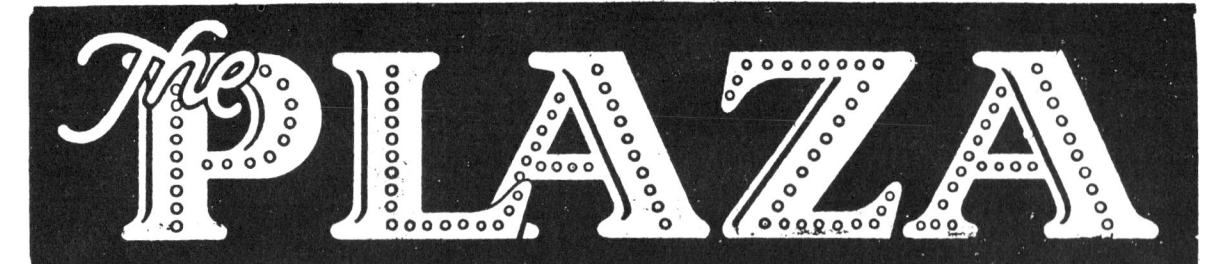

SOUTH ST., CHICHESTER. 'Phone 208. Proprietors: County Cinemas, Ltd. Manager: Albert C. Batt.

To-day (Wednesday). "The Misleading Lady" (CLAUDETTE COLBERT.)

THURSDAY, JANUARY 19th, for three Days.

JACKIE COOPER
IN
DIVORCE in the FAMILY
with
CONRAD NAGEL — LOIS WILSON — LEWIS STONE.

MONDAY, JANUARY 16th, for three days.   DOUBLE FEATURE.

TALLULAH BANKHEAD
IN
THUNDER BELOW
ALSO
Back to Nature.

BARGAIN MATINEES DAILY at 2.30 p.m.   Three Prices Only.
Bank Holidays excepted.   7d., 9d. and 1/- (Children under 14 half-price).

Balcony, 1/6; Stalls, 1/4, 1/-, 9d. and 7d. (including Tax).
1/6 and 1/4 Seats bookable in advance.

95

YOUR WINDOW ON THE LIVING PAST

Make friends with the monthly magazine that opens up a new window on the past in Hampshire, West Sussex and the Isle of Wight. No heavy historical lectures here – it's full of lively articles, fascinating photographs, and a blend of ancient and modern local history that has won it a firm following among thousands of readers.

Yesterday is the magazine that puts a human face on history, that shows you how our forefathers lived and worked. Its full-colour features explore the old crafts and transport of yesteryear, backed up by the reminiscences of people who were there.

Yesterday – the magazine that brings the past to life.

ON SALE MONTHLY – £1.20